Irenaeus of Lyons on Baptism and Eucharist:

Selected texts with Introduction, Translation and Annotation

by David N. Power

THE ALCUIN CLUB and the GROUP FOR RENEWAL OF WORSHIP (GROW)

The Alcuin Club, which exists to promote the study of Christian liturgy in general and of Anglican liturgy in particular, traditionally published a single volume annually for its members. This ceased in 1986. Similarly, GROW was responsible from 1975 to 1986 for the quarterly 'Grove Liturgical Studies'. Since the beginning of 1987 the two have sponsored a Joint Editorial Board to produce quarterly 'Joint Liturgical Studies', details of which are to be found at the end of this Study. Both also produce separate publications and these too are described in the end pages.

THE COVER PICTURE

shows some text of Irenaeus

First Impression June 1991
ISSN 0951-2667
ISBN 1 85174 180 1

CONTENTS

THE EDITOR

David N. Power was born in Dublin, Ireland, in 1932 and educated there by the Christian Brothers. He entered the Missionary Oblates of Mary Immaculate in 1949 and after studies in Rome was ordained a priest in 1956. He obtained a Doctorate in Sacred Theology from the Pontifical Liturgical Institute of Saint Anselm, Rome, in 1968. He has taught systematic theology and liturgy in the Oblate Scholasticate, Ireland, in the Milltown Institute for Philosophy and Theology, Dublin, and at the Gregorian University and the University of Saint Thomas Aquinas in Rome. Since 1977 he has been in the department of theology at The Catholic University of America, Washington, U.S.A.

His publications include: *Ministers of Christ and his Church. A Theology of Priesthood* (Geoffrey Chapman, London: 1969); *Christian Priest: Elder and Prophet* (Sheed & Ward, London: 1973); *Gifts That Differ: Lay Ministries Established and Unestablished* (Pueblo Publishing Company, New York: second edition, 1985); *Unsearchable Riches: The Symbolic Nature of Liturgy* (Pueblo Publishing Company, New York: 1984); *The Sacrifice We Offer: the Tridentine Dogma and its Reinterpretation* (T. & T. Clark, Ltd., Edinburgh: 1987); *Worship: Culture and Theology* (The Pastoral Press, Washington, D.C.: 1991).

He has been on the editorial board of the international theological journal, *Concilium*, since 1969 and has co-edited its issues on liturgy. His articles have appeared in *The Heythrop Journal*, *The Way*, *Worship*, *Doctrine and Life*, *Ecclesia Orans*, *Chicago Studies*, *Pastoral Music*, *East Asian Pastoral Review*, *La Vie Spirituelle*, *La Maison-Dieu*.

Introduction

For liturgical scholars, the interest of the writings of Irenaeus can be expressed in his words from the treatise *Against the Heresies* IV.18.5: 'our opinion agrees with the eucharist, and the eucharist in turn confirms our opinion'. This is an early formulation of the viewpoint expressed later in the adage, *'lex orandi lex credendi'*, by which writers note the relation between the doctrine of the faith and the rites of worship.

Irenaeus was of the third generation of Christian teachers, who had known some of the disciples of the apostles and their companions. A presbyter of the church of Lyons, he became its bishop in succession to Saint Pothinus in 177/178 c.e. He died around 202 and is venerated as a martyr. His writings are essentially a defense against gnostic heresies of the rule of faith handed down by the elders, or in other words of the apostolic doctrine. What he says of sacramental rites is relatively sparse, but it is of interest on two scores. First, it gives some information about the rites and doctrine of eucharist and baptism in the early Christian centuries for which little exists by way of liturgical texts. Second, it shows where sacrament and the rule of faith relate to one another. Something will be said on both of these scores by way of conclusion, after a reading of the texts.

The two works of Irenaeus from which excerpts are here presented are the *Proof of the Apostolic Teaching* and *Against the Heresies*. Unfortunately, the original Greek text of neither work is extant and hence English translations are done from versions in a variety of ancient languages other than Greek.

Though the *Proof of the Apostolic Teaching* is written in the formof a letter, it seems to have been intended as a guideline to pre-baptismal catechesis based on what Irenaeus calls' the rule of faith handed down by the elders'. In contemporary terms, it would be said that it is an exposition of the creed, with generous appeal to the scriptures. The creed in question is that given in the baptismal rite. The exposition is offered by Irenaeus in clear response to gnostic teaching about creation and redemption.

Irenaeus shows a similar preoccupation with the gnostics of his time who perverted the Christian faith in his work *Against the Heresies*. Much of our information about gnosticism comes from church writers, who obviously were not overconcerned with objectivity in what they said of their opponents. Nonetheless, some idea of what these opponents taught emerges.

In general, the gnostics who were accused of perverting Christian truth believed that they had passed beyond the teaching of the apostles and found some higher knowledge, through special revelation. There were many groups, brought together by a variety of prophets, so that their teachings were varied. There do seem to have been, however, some common tenets among them.

In what they taught of the relation of the world to God, they held to a great void. This was filled with aeons who emanated from the divine being. These were responsible for the creation of the world. Through this doctrine of aeons, the gnostics addressed the problem of matter and spirit, good and evil. They associated evil with matter and attributed its origins to one creative principle, whereas they associated good with spirit, its origins being attributed to another creative principle. The apostolic teaching on both creation and redemption is thus perverted. The doctrine of the Word is central to right faith, since it demonstrates that creation is by the one God through the Word, and that redemption of humankind comes about through the Word's taking on human nature in its complete reality of spirit and flesh.

The response of Irenaeus is to appeal against the heretics to the rule of faith, handed down by the elders and guaranteed by the bishops of churches founded by apostles or their disciples. This is particularly important for right teaching on creation, incarnation and redemption. Sometimes, as in the texts presented in this study, he finds corroboration of this rule of faith in the rites of baptism and eucharist. He also supports Christian sacrament in opposition to the rituals practised by gnostic groups. The correct understanding of these Christian rites, especially eucharist, also involves right doctrine. The elements of doctrine most pertinent to right liturgical practice are those of creation, incarnation and resurrection of the flesh.

The gnostic teachings were many and varied and in the course of his work Irenaeus addresses many of them. In those passages, however, where he contrasts Christian rites of baptism and eucharist with gnostic rites, he appears to have the followers of Marcus particularly in view. This is understandable, since the prophet Marcus gathered his followers from the Rhone valley, where Irenaeus himself was bishop.

Amongst religious practices, sacrifice is common to many bodies and peoples, and Christianity also claims its sacrifice. There is both an apologetic and a doctrinal factor to this claim. If they were without sacrifice, Christians would seem to be without religion. In claiming to practise it, their meaning and intent needs to be clear. Where there is a doctrine of intermediaries between God and the world sacrifice is addressed to them, and has as much to do with their placation as with nobility of spirit.For Irenaeus, it is the eucharist which gives a sound understanding of sacrifice in the context of right understanding about God's relation to the world, in creation through the Word and in redemption through the Word made flesh.

The text of the *Proof of the Apostolic Preaching* is known to us principally from an Armenian version. The English text used here is taken from an Armenian scholar, Joseph P. Smith, who dates it towards the end of the second century while Irenaeus was bishop of Lyons. The translation is published as volume 16 of the series, *Ancient Christian Writers*.

The text of *Against the Heresies* has come down to us principally in an ancient Latin version. Some of the original Greek remains in quotations by Epiphanius of Salamis in his work known as *Haereses*, by Hippolytus in his treatise *Philosophoumena*, and in the *Sacra Parallela* attributed to John Damascene. There are also fragments of Syrian and Armenian versions. Recently, the collection *Sources Chrétiennes* has offered a reconstruction of the Greek text for the entire work, along with the Latin and a French translation. For the English version of pertinent texts used in this study, the basis was provided by the collection, *The Ante-Nicene Fathers*, volume 1. The Latin text and the Greek reconstruction were consulted, as well as other English translations noted in the bibliography, and the French translation given in *Sources Chrétiennes.*

The texts presented in this study have to do with baptism and with eucharist. Commentary is offered by way of footnote. At the end, conclusions are drawn about the rites and doctrine of both sacraments, and about the relation between worship and doctrine.

1. Baptismal Texts

THE PROOF OF THE APOSTOLIC TEACHING[1]

BAPTISM AND THE RULE OF FAITH[2]

3: First of all the rule of faith admonishes us to remember that we have received baptism for remission of sins in the name of God the Father, and in the name of Jesus Christ, and in the Holy Spirit of God; and that this baptism is the seal[3] of eternal life and is rebirth unto God, that we be no more children of mortal beings, but of the eternal and everlasting God; and that the eternal and everlasting One is God, and is above all creatures, and that all things whatsoever are subject to him; and that what is subject to him was all made by him, so that God is not ruler and Lord of what is another's, but of his own, and all things are God's[4]; that God, therefore, is the almighty, and all things whatsoever are from God.

---

[1] The two texts taken from this work associate the rule of faith with baptism. According to the *Apostolic Tradition* 21, the profession of faith was made by the candidates in response to the bishop when they entered the baptismal pool and was connected with the water immersion. On the other hand, Justin Martyr, *Apologia* I, 61,10-11, seems to indicate an invocation in the name of the three persons over the candidate while in the pool. According to *Didascalia* 16, this latter was also the practice in Syria. In elaborating here on the rule of faith given in baptism, Irenaeus is generally thought to refer to an invocation of the names of the three persons over the person in the pool, rather than to a profession of faith made by the candidate. In either case, this is the norm or rule of faith set down by the elders which serves Irenaeus as a point of departure for a baptismal catechesis, on the basis of which he frequently argues against gnostic tenets about creation through intermediaries rather than through the Word of God.

[2] What is normative for faith is what is handed down by the elders and professed in baptism, and thus sanctioned by both tradition and ritual. Compare *Against the Heresies* I.9.4 on the 'rule of the truth which is received by means of baptism'.

[3] The Greek word used is probably *sphragis*. In the time of Irenaeus, in some churches along with water baptism there was an anointing with oil, but he himself does not appear to have known of this rite. In any case, there was no conceptual distinction between baptism and consignation, or confirmation as it came to be called in the west. The words 'baptism' and 'seal' refer to the entire service, whether it involved only water immersion or both rites. Irenaeus here gives an eschatological explanation for the word, which signifies that baptism is a guarantee of eternal life.

[4] The two preceding affirmations are directed against the gnostic teaching of a creation through beings which emanate from the first principle and are inferior to it. This is often connected with a further tenet of a dual creative principle, one of matter and the other of spirit, all evil being connected with matter. Irenaeus affirms that the creation of all things in supreme freedom by the one almighty and supreme God is inherent to the apostolic teaching and rule of faith.

6: And this is the drawing up of our faith[1], the foundation of the building,and the consolidation of a way of life. God the Father, uncreated, beyond grasp, invisible, one God the maker of all; this is the first and foremost article of our faith[2]. But the second article is the Word of God, the Son of God, Christ Jesus our Lord, who was shown forth by the prophets according to the design of their prophecy and according to the manner in which the Father disposed; and through him were made all things whatsoever[3]. He also, in the end of times, for the recapitulation of all things[4], is become human among humans, visible and tangible, in order to abolish death and bring to light life, and bring about the communion of God and human[5]. And the third article is the Holy Spirit, through whom the prophets prophesied and the patriarchs were taught about God and the just were led in the path of justice, and who in the end of times has been poured forth in a new manner upon humanity over all the earth renewing humans to God.

---

[1] The Greek word is probably *taxis*, which besides indicating what is normative also connotes the idea of economy.

[2] This is the first article professed by the candidate at baptism, joined with the invocation of the name of the Father. It associates creation with belief in God the Father. This is contrary to the gnostic tenet that creation is not from the first principle. Further down, Irenaeus adds that creation is *through* the Word, not therefore making of it a separate principle of creation but one with the Father.

[3] Irenaeus allows of no distinction in the origin of spiritual and material beings. Furthermore, by associating the Word with creation he affirms its oneness and equality with the Father.

[4] This is an expression particularly associated with Irenaeus, meaning bringing all things back into their head and source, the Word. Though sin results in a dispersal, the work of redemption is to restore the order, unity and intent of creation.

[5] Though Irenaeus here comments on the baptismal formula, his words resonate with imagery found in early paschal homilies and later in the eucharistic prayer of the *Apostolic Tradition* 4. It has been suggested that his work had a direct influence on the composition of this prayer. With this passage, compare:

Against the Heresies II.20.3:

'Our Lord by his passion destroyed death and dispersed error, and put an end to corruption, and destroyed ignorance, while he manifested life and revealed truth, and bestowed the gift of incorruption'.

Apostolic Tradition (eucharistic prayer as translated by the International Commission for English in the Liturgy):

'Of his own free choice he was handed over to his passion in order to make an end to death and to shatter the claims of the evil one, to trample underfoot the powers of hell and to lead the righteous into light; to establish the boundaries of death and to manifest the resurrection'.

AGAINST THE HERESIES

I.21.1-2: MARCOSIAN VIEWS ON BAPTISM AND REDEMPTION[1]

1. It happens that their the Marcosians' tradition respecting redemption is invisible and incomprehensible, as being the mother of things which are incomprehensible and invisible; and on this account, since it is fluctuating, it is impossible simply and all at once to make known its nature, for every one of them hands down just as his own inclination prompts. Thus there are as many schemes of redemption as there are teachers of these mystical opinions. And when we come to refute them, we shall show in its fitting place, that such people have been instigated by Satan to a denial of that baptism which is regeneration to God, and thus to a renunciation of the whole faith.[2]

2. ... For the baptism instituted by the visible Jesus [according to the Marcosians] was for the remission of sins, but the redemption brought in by that Christ who descended upon him, was for perfection; and they allege that the former is animal, but the latter spiritual. And the baptism of John was proclaimed with a view to repentance, but the redemption by Christ was brought in for the sake of perfection And to this he refers when he says, 'And I have another baptism to be baptized with, and I hasten eagerly towards it [Luke 12.50][3]...'[4]

II.22.4[1]: THE AGE OF CANDIDATES FOR BAPTISM.

Being thirty years old when he came to be baptized, and then possessing the age of a teacher, Christ came to Jerusalem, so that he might be properly

---

[1] In this chapter, Irenaeus describes the various views of the Marcosians regarding baptism and redemption, as well as their rites of redemption, which they distinguish from baptism. This is connected with their view that the superior being, Christ, descended on the man, Jesus, when he was thirty years of age. They then say that Jesus gave a baptism in water for the remission of sins, but that the redemption which is regeneration is in Christ and is for the perfect. Some have rites to celebrate this redemption, but essentially it is a mystic union. Irenaeus upholds the one catholic baptism for the remission of sins and for regeneration.

[2] Here he has in mind the distinction between remission of sins and regeneration proposed by the heretics. Since this distinction involves a whole set of errors regarding God and the incarnation of the Word and the gift of the Spirit, it is an error which involves a renunciation of the whole faith.

[3] Apparently the heretics associate the baptism instituted by *Jesus* with his own baptism by John in the Jordan, no doubt taking this as his institution of baptism for repentance and the remission of sins. The baptism and redemption by *Christ* are then distinguished from this.

[4] In the rest of the chapter I.21.3-5 Irenaeus describes some of the rites which the heretics associate with the redemption of the perfect. These are a mixture of water rites and anointings, with invocations of the mysterious powers.

[5] The gnostics held that Christ made his appearance at thirty years of age at the baptism in the Jordan, descending on the man, Jesus, that he preached for only one year and suffered in the twelfth month after his baptism. They connected this with their doctrine of thirty Aeons that emanate from the Pleroma. Holding for the incarnation of the Word in the birth of Jesus, Irenaeus argues here that Jesus and Christ are one and the same, and that he passed through every age, from infancy onward, thus sanctifying every age.

acknowledged by all as a teacher . . . Being a teacher, therefore, he also possessed the age of a teacher, not despising or evading any condition of humanity, nor evading any condition of humanity, nor setting aside in himself that law which he had appointed for the human race, but sanctifying every age, by that period corresponding to it which belonged to himself. For he came to save all through means of himself—all, I say, who through him are born again[1] to God—infants, and children, and boys, and youths, and the old . . .

III.17.1-3: THE GIFT OF THE SPIRIT[2]

1: . . . the Spirit of God as a dove descended upon [Jesus]; this Spirit of whom it was declared by Isaiah, 'And the Spirit of God shall rest upon him [Isaiah 11.2]', as I have already said. And again, 'the Spirit of the Lord is upon me, because he has anointed me [Isaiah 61.1]'. That is the Spirit of whom the Lord declares, 'For it is not you that speak, but the Spirit of your Father which speaks in you [John 16.7]'. And again, giving to the disciples the power of regeneration into God[3], he said to them, 'Go and teach all nations, baptizing them in the name of the Father, and of the Son, and of the Holy Spirit [Matt. 28.19] . . .'

2: . . . For as a compact lump of dough cannot be formed of dry wheat without fluid matter, nor can a loaf possess unity, so, in like manner, neither could we, being many, be made one in Christ Jesus without the water from heaven. And as dry earth does not bring forth unless it receives moisture, in like manner we also, being originally a dry tree, could never have brought forth fruit unto life without the voluntary rain from above. For our bodies have received unity among themselves by means of that laver which leads to incorporation; but our souls by means of the Spirit[4] . . .

3: . . . we have need of the dew of God[5], that we be not consumed by fire, nor be rendered unfruitful[6], and that where we have an accuser there we may also have

[1] The phrase 'born again to God' is a clear reference to baptism. Though his was an age in which chiefly adults were baptized, Irenaeus indicates here that he knew of the baptism of infants and children.

[2] In this chapter, Irenaeus treats of the baptism of Jesus in the Jordan. The gnostics held that the superior being, Christ, descended upon the man, Jesus. In response, Irenaeus shows that it was the Spirit who descended upon the Word made flesh, that same Spirit which is given to those saved in him at baptism. Hence themes affecting the meaning of Christian baptism are mixed into the discourse on Christ's baptism.

[3] Note here the imagery of regeneration to denote what happens through baptism. Note also the use of the preposition with the accusative, *eis Theov,* 'into God'.

[4] Irenaeus is here using several images expressing the union of many in one to designate the effect of the gift of the Spirit in baptism. Note how with the image of incorporation, or union with a body, he combines both the material and the spiritual. That the human body and not only the soul is saved is of constant interest to Irenaeus, and here he speaks of the external unity of the church as a unity of many bodies, to which external unity corresponds inner union in the Spirit.

[5] Irenaeus has just referred to the dew on the fleece in the story of Gideon, Judges 6, 36-40.

[6] Here we find a theme common in Irenaeus. The worship of God is not rooted in a need on God's part, but it is a gift to human beings that allows them to show their own relation to God, in a worship that harmonizes with good works. The metaphor is that of a well-cared tree producing good fruit.

an advocate, the Lord commending to the Holy Spirit his own human race, on whom he had shown compassion when it fell among thieves, and bound up its wounds, giving two royal coins; so that we, receiving the image and superscription of the Father and the Son, might cause the coins entrusted to us to be fruitful, counting out the increase to the Lord[1].

[1] Irenaeus uses the story of the Samaritan who tended the wounded man and paid for him at the inn with two coins Luke 10.29-37 to illustrate the gift of the Spirit in baptism. Using the idea of the image imprinted on a coin, he notes that by the Spirit the Christian receives the image of both Father and Son, the two images typified by the two coins.

2. Eucharistic Texts

AGAINST THE HERESIES

I.13.2 THE EUCHARISTIC RITES OF THE MARCOSIANS[1]

Feigning to give thanks[2] for the cup mixed with wine and drawing out at length the word of invocation[3], he makes the cup appear purple and red, so that Grace[4], who is among the superior beings, may be thought to drip her own blood into that cup through means of his invocation, and that those who are present might greatly desire to taste of that drink, so that Grace, who is invoked by the magician, might drip on them too. Again, handing mixed cups to the women he commands them to give thanks [or make eucharist] in his presence.[5] And when this has been done, he himself brings forth another cup much larger than the one eucharistized by the deluded woman[6], and pours from the smaller cup, which

---

[1] Irenaues is here describing the rites of the gnostic followers of Marcus, known as the Marcosians. Of late there has been renewed interest in this description, because of what it may confirm about early orthodox liturgies in Judeo-Christian churches. Though Marcus perverts the rite, what he does has some basis in authentic celebration. Thus this text is compared with reconstructions of Judeo-Christian liturgies based chiefly on the *Didache* 9, the seventh book of the *Apostolic Constitutions*, some texts from the apocryphal acts, and their comparison with Jewish traditions of blessing.

The Greek text for this passage is cited in Epiphanius. *Haer*. xxxiv.1 and Hippolytus, *Philosoph*. vi.39.40.

[2] The Greek verb is *eucharistein*, usually translated as 'to give thanks'. It may here however be a more generic term for blessing, signifying a variant form of prayer that blesses God, either with praise, with thanksgiving, or with invocation. The Jewish blessing of God or *berakah* allows for all three forms, but the constant is the doxology of the divine name.

[3] The Greek term is *epiclesis*, usually associated with petition and the invocation of a name in whose power the favour is asked. Some early prayers allow for an invocation of the Word and in speaking of the prayer Irenaeus himself has the invocation of the name of the Word Incarnate in view. Later the word is used to designate the invocation of the Spirit over the sacramental elements of bread, wine, oil and water, or over persons. With Irenaeus, however, we should not expect to find a clearly developed liturgical vocabulary, nor a developed theology of the Spirit. Neither prayer forms nor vocabulary had in his time reached the clarity and stability to which we have become accustomed.

[4] The Greek word used is *charis*, and it is used here as a proper name for one of the intermediary beings of the gnostic hierarchy.

[5] The exercise of such a prayer role by women used to be seen as one of the traits of heterodox bodies. Now that New Testament studies have shown the leadership of women in early house-churches and the presence of women among the prophets of early times, it is no longer clear that women were excluded from invoking liturgical blessings in ecclesial assemblies. For some, the Marcosian liturgy in this regard may simply reflect an orthodox practice, later discontinued and prohibited.

[6] The text here slips into the singular, having used the plural further up.

has been made eucharist by the woman, into the one which he himself brought forward, saying over it[1]: May that Grace[2] who is before all things, unthinkable and unspeakable, fill your inner self and increase in you her knowledge, planting the mustard seed in good ground [cf. Matt. 13.31]. And saying such words and driving the wretched woman to madness, he appears to have worked wonders, when the larger cup was filled from the smaller, even to overflowing. And performing other similar acts, he deceived many and drew them after himself.

IV.17.1-4: ON THE SACRIFICES OF THE LAW[3]

17.1: Moreover, the prophets indicate in the fullest manner that it was not because he needed their service, but on their own account, that God prescribed the observances found in the Law. In turn, as we will show, the Lord clearly taught that God did not need their oblation but prescribed it for the sake of the human being who offers it[4].

When he saw them [the people] neglecting righteousness[5], and turning from the love of God, and nonetheless thinking that God could be propitiated[6] through sacrifices and other figurative observances, Samuel said to them: 'The Lord does not desire holocausts and sacrifices, but rather that the Lord's voice

---

[1] The form of the following prayer fits into the genre of blessing in Jewish and Judeo-Christian context. Though we are now accustomed to consider blessing prayers composed of thanksgiving and invocation, with the proper doxology invocation alone could constitute a blessing. There are several examples of this for the eucharist in the apocryphal acts, of Thomas, Peter and John respectively.

[2] In prayers of Judeo-Christian communities, one finds invocation of the Name (i.e. of God as revealed in the name of Jesus or the works of grace), or the Mother or the Dove (both of these a naming of God as the source of blessings on creatures). As noted above, later such invocation developed into an invocation of the name of the Holy Spirit.

[3] Having considered the sacrifices of the gnostics and pagan sacrifices, both linked with belief in intermediaries between God and creatures, Irenaeus sets out to consider the sacrifices established by God, beginning with the sacrifices of the Law. This disquisition on the reason for sacrifice and on the proper way of offering it, is important background to his discussion of the sacrifice of the new covenant, the eucharist.

[4] Irenaeus clearly lays down the principle that the reason for ritual observance, particularly sacrifice, is to be found in human nature, not in any need for worship on God's part. This is taught both by the prophets and by the Lord, i.e. Jesus Christ.

[5] The Latin word is *justitia*, which translates the Greek *dikaiosune*. It refers to that in the human person which results from God's justifying action, but also connotes the right conduct that follows and is demanded by the Law. Hence the English word 'righteousness' to convey both senses of the word.

[6] In understanding sacrifice in general and the eucharist in particular, much hangs on the use of the word 'propitiate'. In ordinary usage it could mean to render satisfaction for wrong done, or to assuage one who has been angered. It may well be used in that sense here, indicating the mistaken notion of the people that they could avert God's eyes from their wrong-doing by offering sacrifices. When Irenaeus uses propitiation of Christ's death or of the eucharist, he makes it clear that this has nothing to do with divine anger but that such sacrifice is rendered rather out of divine compassion. On Christ's death as propitiation, cf. *Against the Heresies* IV.16 (ANF I 471).

might be heard. Behold a ready obedience prevails over sacrifice, and attention to God's voice over the fat of rams [1 Sam 15.22]. David also said: 'Sacrifice and oblation you did not want, but you have perfected my ears, holocausts for sin you have not asked [Psalm 51.17]'. By this he taught that God desires obedience, for it is this which saves them, not sacrifices and holocausts, which avail nothing towards righteousness, and in this he prophesied the new covenant . . .[1].

17.2: It was not, as many venture to say, like a human being moved [by anger], that God rejected their sacrifices, but it was out of compassion for their blindness and in order to teach the nature of true sacrifice by whose offering they shall propitiate[2] God, so that they can receive life as a divine gift. As it is said elsewhere: 'The sacrifice to God is an afflicted heart: a sweet savour to God is a heart glorifying the One who formed it[3]. . .'

IV.17.4-18.6. THE EUCHARIST

17.4[4]: From all of this it is evident that God did not seek sacrifices and holocausts from them, but the faith and obedience and righteousness which bring salvation. As God teaches them through Hosea the prophet: 'I desire mercy rather than sacrifice and the knowledge of God more than holocausts [Hosea 6.6]'. Besides, the Lord also exhorted them to the same effect, saying: 'But if you had known what this means: I wish mercy and not sacrifice, you would never have condemned the innocent [Matt. 12.7]'. In this he bears witness to the prophets that they preached the truth, accusing his hearers of the guilt of their own foolishness.

17.5: The Lord gave directions to his disciples to offer first-fruits to God from God's own creatures, not as though God stood in need of them, but that they themselves may be neither unfruitful nor ungrateful'.[5] Thus, he took the bread, which comes from creation, and he gave thanks, saying: 'This is my

---

[1] Irenaeus continues to show the priority of obedience over sacrifice, with quotations from Psalms 39.7; 50.18-19; 49.9-13, 14-15; Isaiah 1.10, 16-18.

[2] Anger is clearly absent from propitiation in this case. The word might well be translated 'draw near', signifying some action on humanity's part by which out of divine generosity it can make some movement towards righting relationships with God.

[3] As they stand, these words are not found in any scriptural passage. They possibly refer to Psalm 50 [51].

In what follows (17.2 and 17.3) the point continues to be made about the compassion which God extends to the people, showing them the way to salvation, even though their sacrifices were unpleasing to him because of their false motivation.

[4] This concludes the discussion of Old Testament observances and leads into the eucharist.

[5] The reason for sacrifice is here found in human nature. It allows human beings to show their gratitude, by offering the first-fruits of that creation of which they are themselves a part. In the old dispensation, it was literally the first-fruits of harvest or flock that were offered each year, signifying the dedication of all fruit, all work and all life to God. In the new covenant, the bread and wine of each eucharist have the symbolic role of first-fruits of all of creation.

Body'. He did likewise with the cup, which is part of the creation to which we ourselves belong, declaring it to be his blood[1], and [so] he taught the new offering of the new covenant. This is the offering which the church received from the apostles and which it offers throughout the whole world, to God who provides us with nourishment, the first-fruits of divine gifts in this new covenant.[2]

Of this offering, among the prophets, Malachi had spoken beforehand in these terms: 'I have no pleasure in you, says the Lord almighty, and I will not accept sacrifice from your hands. For from the rising of the sun even to its setting my name is glorified among the nations, and in every place incense is offered to my name, and a pure sacrifice; for my name is great among the nations, says the Lord almighty [Mal. 1,10-11][3]'. By these words, he shows in the plainest manner that the former people shall cease to make offering to God, but that in every place sacrifice shall be offered to God, one that is pure, and that God's name is glorified among the nations.

17.6: But what is the name which is glorified among the nations, if not that of our Lord, through whom the Father is glorified, and humankind is glorified?[4] And because it is the name of the Father's own Son, and was made by the Father, he calls it his own.[5] Just as a king, if he himself paints a portrait of his son, is right in calling this likeness his own, for both these reasons, that is, because it is of his own son and because he himself made it, so also the Father acknowledges that the name of Jesus Christ, which is glorified in the church, throughout the world, is his own, both because it is the name of his Son, and because he himself

---

[1] There are different interpretations of this sentence, indicating differences in understanding of the eucharistic action. Some think that it is the blood (and thus also the body) of Christ which is offered, this being the first-fruits of the new creation. A more likely interpretation is that for Irenaeus it is indeed bread and wine, first-fruits of the earth, which are offered, but they are offered with thanksgiving and invocation of the name of Christ, and so, through this offering/thanksgiving, become the body and blood of Christ. This offering with commemorative thanksgiving would then be the new offering of the new covenant.

[2] Irenaeus here seems to be playing with the image of first-fruits. In this case, the first-fruits of the new creation which are God's gift to human beings for their nourishment are the sustenance of the body and blood of Christ. Thus, when humans offer bread and wine, the first-fruits of creation, with thanksgiving in the name of Christ, they receive as nourishment the first-fruits of the new creation, which are the body and blood of Christ.

[3] This text is already used of the eucharist in *Didache* 14,1-2 and by Justin, *Dial* 116.3:117.2. It is used by Christian writers both to underline the purity of heart and the praise of God's name with which the New Testament sacrifice is offered, and as a polemic against the Jews, who with the destruction of the temple in Jerusalem had ceased to offer sacrifices. This polemic is less intense in Irenaeus than in other writers.

[4] This is a typical theme for Irenaeus, that in humankind's glorification there lies the glory of God.

[5] The name intended here is probably the name of Lord, which God gave to Jesus Christ, the Son. It is the name of the Son, and a name which the Father made in raising him up from the dead. What is also included is the idea that Jesus Christ is the image of the Father, so that in his name the name of the Father is made manifest.

inscribed it, giving it for the salvation of humankind [cf. Acts 4.12]. Since therefore the name of the Son belongs properly to the Father, and since the church makes offering through Jesus Christ to God almighty[1], Malachi says well on both grounds 'and in every place incense is offered to my name, and a pure sacrifice'. Now John declares in the Apocalypse that the incense is the prayer of the saints [Rev 5.8].

18.1: The oblation of the church, therefore, which the Lord taught should be offered throughout the world, is accounted with God a pure sacrifice. It is acceptable, not because God needs sacrifice from us, but because those who offer sacrifice are themselves glorified in what they offer, if the gift be accepted. For it is through a gift that honour and affection are shown to a king, and this is indeed the gift of which the Lord, wishing us to offer in all simplicity and innocence, says: 'When therefore you offer your gift at the altar, you remember that your brother or sister has anything against you,leave your gift at the altar, and go first to be reconciled to your brother or sister, and then returning you shall offer your gift [Matt. 5.23-24]'.[2] It is necessary therefore to offer the first-fruits of creation to God, as Moses said: 'You shall not appear empty-handed in the sight of the Lord your God [Deut. 16.16]. Showing gratitude in those things by which they are themselves gratified, human beings receive that honour which comes from God'.[3]

18.2: And oblations as a class of action have not been done away with: for there were oblations there, just as there are oblations here, sacrifices among the people as there are sacrifices in the church. It is only the kind of oblation which is changed, inasmuch as it is not anymore offered by slaves but by the free.[4] For the Lord is one and the same[5], but the character of a servile oblation is peculiar to

---

[1] The Latin here has *'in'* almighty God, but translators usually prefer *'to'* as more in keeping with the sense of the passage. The eucharistic ritual here described is the offering of bread and wine with thanksgiving, through the invocation of the name of Jesus as Saviour and Lord. To offer in this name is to honour it, and to honour it is to honour and make sacrifice to the Father, who gave him this name. It is by the same token the glorification of those human beings who make the offering, and invoke the name in which they are saved.

[2] This text is used to the same effect in *Didache* 14,1. It shows the importance of a pure conscience, or of obedience to the commandments of the new covenant regarding reconciliation, in those who offer the sacrifice of the eucharist in the church assembly.

[3] Following the Armenian version of the text, some translate this differently, introducing a reference to sin and its reparation: 'man, being accounted pleasing to God in those things in which he has been displeasing, receives that honour which comes from God'. In both translations, the text requires an offering of bread and wine as the first-fruits of creation. According to the translation adopted, these stand either for all the gifts in which humans have been blessed by God, or for those gifts which they have abused in sinning.

[4] Irenaeus looks upon oblation and sacrifice as so much a part of human nature, that they are found in both testaments. The radical difference in the sacrifice of the new covenant lies in the graced existence of those who offer, for by the grace of Christ they have been freed from sin and freed to do good.

[5] This is an important point against some of the gnostics, who attributed the Old Testament to one creative principle and the New Testament to another.

itself, as is also that of the offering of the free, established in order that, even through the oblations, an indication of freedom might be shown. For with God, nothing is without purpose, nothing is without signification or design. And for this reason the people had indeed the tithes of their goods consecrated to the Lord, but those who received freedom set apart all they have for the Lord's purposes, giving joyfully and freely even when they have less[1], since they have the hope of greater things, as that poor widow put all her substance into the treasury of God [cf. Lk. 21.1-4].

18.3: For at the beginning[2] God looked with favour on the gifts of Abel, because he offered with singlemindedness and righteousness, but God had no regard for the sacrifice of Cain, because through jealousy and malice he harboured division against his brother in his heart. This is what God noted, reproving his hidden thoughts: 'Though you make offering correctly, yet if you do not share rightly, have you not sinned? Be at rest [cf. Gen. 4.7][3], since God is not appeased by sacrifice. For if some endeavour to offer a sacrifice which is clean, correct and legal according to outward appearances, while not sharing that fellowship with their neighbours which is due, and having no fear of God in their hearts, God is not deceived by that sacrifice which is outwardly correct but hides sin within. Such offering does them no good, but what is wanted is the giving up of the evil conceived within, lest the sin by means of a hypocritical action makes of the giver one's own murderer. Because of this the Lord said: 'Woe to you, scribes and pharisees, hypocrites, for you are like whitened sepulchres. For the sepulchre appears beautiful outside, but within is full of the bones of the dead and of all manner of uncleanness. Even so, you outwardly appear righteous to human eyes, but inside you are full of wickedness and hypocrisy [Matt. 23.27-28]. For while they were thought to make offering correctly in outward appearances, within themselves they harboured a jealousy like that of Cain; therefore they slew the Just One, slighting the counsel of the Word, just as Cain had done.[4] To

---

[1] There is some obscurity in the text at this point. Another possible translation is: giving what is little in light of their greater hope, where the contrast is between the little that humans can give and the greatness of that for which they hope. Irenaeus contrasts the tithing of the Old Testament with the gift of one's whole self made possible by the grace of Christ. In this way, he joins the use of the term *sacrifice* used in the New Testament to designate the Christian life and Christian actions, with its use for the eucharist. The offering of bread and wine made in invocation of Christ's name and with thanksgiving, truly expresses the oblation of oneself and one's whole life in communion with Jesus Christ.

[2] Though the Latin reads *ab*, the sense seems to be *at* or *in*, rather than *from* the beginning.

[3] The reference to God's rest here and below as a symbol of innocence and justice, recalls the use of this motif in Hebrews 3 and 4.

[4] The comparison of the death of Jesus with the killing of Abel goes back to Hebrews 12.24 and is common in early Christian literature. As in the Roman Canon, it underlines the innocence or justice of Christ, contrasting this with the sinfulness of those for whom he gave his life.

him God had said, 'Be at rest', but he did not consent. Now what else is it to be at rest but to abandon intended violence? And saying similar things to these men, he declares: 'You blind pharisee, cleanse that which is within the cup, that the outside may be clean also [Matt. 23.26]'. And they did not listen to him. For Jeremiah says, 'Behold, neither your eyes nor your heart are good; but in your covetousness you turn to shedding innocent blood, and to injustice, and to acts of homicide [Jer. 22.17].' And again Isaiah says: 'You have taken counsel, but not with me; you have made covenants, not by my spirit [Isaiah 30][1]'. In order, therefore, that their inner wish and thought, being brought to light, may show that God is without blame and works no evil, God being the one who makes known hidden things but not the one who works evil, when Cain was not in the least at rest, God said to him: '(sin) seeks you out, but you must master it [Gen. 4.7]'. In like manner (Jesus) spoke to Pilate: 'You would have no power over me, unless it were given you from above [John 19.11]', thus indicating that God always hands over the just, so that, tested by what they have suffered and endured, they may be approved and accepted[2]; the evil however are rejected, judged by the actions which they have performed. Sacrifices[3], therefore, do not sanctify the human person, but rather it is the dispositions of the offerer which sanctify the sacrifice, if they are pure, and move God to accept it as from a friend. 'But when the sinner', God says, 'slays a calf for me, it is as if it were a dog that is slain.'[4].

18.4: Since then the church offers with singlemindedness, its gift is rightly reckoned a pure sacrifice by God, as Paul says to the Philippians: 'I am replete, having received from Epaphroditus the things sent from you, an odour of sweetness, an acceptable sacrifice, one pleasing to God [Phil. 4.18]'.[5] For it is necessary for us

---

[1] Irenaeus, in going on to speak of the opposition of the leading Pharisees and of Pilate to Jesus, appeals to what is almost a general law, namely, the oppression of the innocent by the unjust. This shows the full extent of Christ's participation in the lot of humankind. Irenaeus is also making the point that evil is from the hearts of human beings, not the work of a divine creation.

[2] This recalls Hebrews 5.8-9: 'Although he was Son, he learned obedience through what he suffered; and being made perfect he became the source of eternal salvation to all who obey him'. As Irenaeus elaborates the theme of the suffering of the just at the hands of the wicked, of which the death of Christ is exemplary, he offers a soteriology of compassion. Though the Word of God, Jesus suffered at the hands of the wicked according to the common pattern realized since Abel, and so he brought salvation into the world.

[3] From these more fulsome considerations on the suffering of the just and the way of salvation, Irenaeus returns to the dispositions of the one offering sacrifice. Note how sacrifice is the expression of a righteous heart, of one who is the friend of God, not an attempt to win propitiation from one offended. Irenaeus deems the attempt to do this latter a perversion of sacrifice.

[4] Though it does not exactly correspond, this may be a reference to Isaiah 66.3.

[5] In ways this is an odd use of a scriptural text, since it puts words used by Paul of himself in God's mouth. Irenaeus's first intention no doubt is to express the joyful acceptance by God of the eucharistic sacrifice. His use of this particular text, odd though it sounds, illustrates further the relation between the sacrifice of good deeds and the sacrifice of the eucharist, since Paul does not hesitate to use this liturgical language of a simple act of charity done by one believer to another.

to make an offering to God and to be found in all things grateful[1] to the Creator, offering the first-fruits of creation to the One who made them, with a pure mind, in faith without hypocrisy, in well-Grounded hope, in fervent love[2] Moreover, the church alone offers this pure oblation to the Creator, offering from God's own creation, with thanksgiving. But the Jews no longer make offering, for their hands are full of blood, since they did not accept the Word through whom which offering is made to God[3].

Nor do the assemblies of the heretics make offering. For some, by maintaining that there is a Father other than the Creator, when they offer to him what belongs to our created world, they portray him as covetous of another's property and desirous of what is not his own. On the other hand, those who assert that our creation was made from degeneracy, ignorance, and suffering, sin against their Father when they offer him the fruits of ignorance, suffering and degeneracy; they rather heap insult on him than offer him thanks[4]. But how can they be sure that the bread over which thanks has been given (which has been eucharistized)[5] is the body of their Lord, and the cup his blood, if they do not call him the Son of the Creator of the world, that is, God's Word[6], through whom the wood fructifies, and the fountains gush forth, and the earth gives first the blade, then the ear, then the full wheat in the ear [Mk. 4.28].

---

[1] Some translations say 'pleasing'. It fits in more readily with the attempt to find a motif of appeasement for sin in sacrifice.

[2] These dispositions of purity of mind, faith, hope and love, sum up all that is said of the disposition of Christians in offering the eucharistic sacrifice.

[3] At this point, Irenaeus joins the common bias against the Jews, associating their loss of sacrificial ritual with their alleged guilt.

[4] Irenaeus is here arguing against the gnostics by way of demonstrating the contradiction between doctrine and practice. What exact eucharistic rites were retained by these assemblies we do not know, since there is no direct testimony. We have seen the description which Irenaeus gives of the rites of the Marcosians. It is likely that some groups retained more of the catholic vocabulary of Father and Son, even while professing creation through intermediaries. Irenaeus here takes two kinds of such teaching into account. On the one hand, he says that if creation is in fact the work of one other than the Father, then it makes him covetous to require that created things be offered to him. On the other hand, if material creation emanates from a principle of evil, offering created things to the Father is an insult and an injury. Behind such argumentation is his own teaching of the rule of faith, that the Father creates all things through his only Word, that material things are essentially good, and so rightly included in the eucharistic offering.

[5] As above, the sense here is that thanksgiving or '*eucharistia*' makes the bread the body and the wine the blood of Christ.

[6] Irenaeus sees no sense in the claim to possess a sacramental body and blood of any being other than the Word and Son. He argues against the gnostic contention of sacramental communion with heavenly intermediaries, to whom they would allow some lordship or dominion over them in their quest for truth.

18.5[1]: Then again, how can they say that the flesh goes to corruption and does not partake of life, when it is nourished by the Lord's body and blood?[2] Therefore, either let them change their opinion or refrain from offering the things just mentioned. But our opinion agrees with the eucharist, and the eucharist in turn confirms our opinion. For we offer to God those things which belong to God, proclaiming fittingly the communion and unity of the flesh and the spirit. For as the bread, which is produced from the earth, when it receives the invocation[3] of God is no longer common bread, but the eucharist[4], consisting of two realities, the earthly and the heavenly[5], so also our bodies, when they receive the eucharist, are no longer corruptible, but have the hope of resurrection. 18.6[6]: Now we make offering to God, not as though to one who stands in need of it, but giving thanks for God's gift[7] and sanctifying what has been created. For even as God has no need of what is ours, so we need to offer something to God, as Solomon says: 'Whoever has pity on the poor lends to God [Prov. 19.17]'. For God, who stands in need of nothing, accepts our good actions so that through them we may have the recompense of God's good things, as our Lord says: 'Come, blessed of my Father, receive the kingdom prepared for you. For I was

---

[1] For this paragraph, a fragment of the original Greek is found in John Damascene, *Sacra Parallela*.

[2] Arguing from the eucharist, Irenaeus is further contesting the idea of a dual creation, especially when it holds for the evil of the material. More important is his own doctrine of the resurrection of the flesh, which he sees confirmed by the eucharistic nourishment of the body with the body and blood of Christ.

[3] The Greek word is *epiclesis*. In this context, the word may well stand for the entire eucharistic prayer. This would be in keeping with the idea,expressed earlier, that the eucharist is the invocation and glorification of the name of Jesus Christ, Word of the Father.

[4] The substantive, *eucharist*, is here used to designate that over which eucharist has been pronounced. At this point, it is' no longer common bread'.

[5] Irenaeus is looking for a way to express the change which comes about in the eucharistized bread. The union of the earthly and heavenly elements may simply mean the bread and wine, which are of earth, and the word, which is the word of the Word of God. It seems, however, that he is implying something further, that is, a union in the eucharist between the risen Lord and the bread, like the union of the earthly and heavenly in the Word made flesh himself. We have to remember that no clear formulation of eucharistic change had yet been worked out and Irenaeus is here simply offering what could be called an analogy of faith. The important thing is that the risen Lord is now present as nourishment for the faithful in this visible and earthly reality of bread, and that this nourishment gives them the assurance and hope of their own resurrection.

[6] This paragraph is noteworthy in that it incorporates the ethical notion of sacrifice, or the offering of good actions, into the understanding of the eucharist. In the early church, the understanding of eucharist as sacrifice developed in parallel with the use of sacrificial terms to explain the Christian life. Ultimately, it is the Christian people which in its union with Christ is itself the sacrifice and the priesthood in which God's glory is manifested and proclaimed.

[7] The Armenian text has 'by means of God's gift'.

hungry, and you gave me to eat; I was thirsty, and you gave me to drink; I was a stranger, and you took me in; I was naked, and you clothed me; I was sick, and you visited me; in prison, and you came to me [Matt. 25.34-36]'. As, therefore, standing in no need of these things, God desires that we should do them, for our benefit lest we be unfruitful, thus the Word, though not in need of them, gave to the people that very precept, to make offerings, that they might learn to serve God. Thus the Word wills that we too should offer a gift at the altar, frequently and without interruption[1].

There is, therefore, an altar in heaven, for towards that place are our prayers and offerings directed. There is also a temple, as John says in the Apocalypse: 'And the temple of God was opened [Rev. 11.19]', as there is a tabernacle, 'For behold', he says, 'the tabernacle in which God will dwell with human beings [Rev. 21.3]'[2].

5.2.2-3: INCARNATION, EUCHARIST, RESURRECTION[3]

5.2.2: Altogether senseless are they who hold God's entire economy in contempt and deny the salvation of the flesh and spurn its regeneration, saying that it is not capable of incorruptibility. Now if this flesh is not saved, neither did the Lord redeem us with his blood, nor is the cup of the eucharist communion in his blood, nor is the bread which we break communion in his body [cf. 1 Cor. 10.6]. For blood comes only from veins and from flesh, and from the rest of human nature, which however the Word truly became, and redeemed us by his blood. Thus the apostle says: 'In whom we have redemption through his blood, and the remission of sins [Col. 1.14]'. And[4] we are his members and are nourished

---

[1] Many images run together in this passage, not clearly or logically sorted out, yet showing how all things in the divine economy belong together. To the image of eternal life as gift through eucharistic nourishment there is joined that of eternal life as recompense for deeds of mercy. To the image of human dependency, there is joined the imagery of fruitfulness in the things commanded by God. To the offering of bread and wine in the eucharist, there is joined the offering of deeds of service by observance of the commandment ofthe new covenant. Irenaeus also points to the unity of the two testaments, by pointing to the Word as the author of both.

The 'frequently and without interruption' probably refers directly to the eucharistic action, but no doubt connotes the offering of good deeds.

[2] The eschatological quality of the eucharist and of the Christian life is here brought out. All sacrifices, works and prayers offered in Christ lead to the end of all sacrifice, which is eternal communion with God in Christ. Cultic terminology can still be employed of heaven, for in this communion there lies the ultimate realization of God's glory through the work of creation.

[3] In this passage, Irenaeus argues for the resurrection of the flesh from the reality of the eucharist. His argument depends on the coherence of the entire economy of creation and redemption. The doctrine of the one creator of all things, material as well as spiritual, the doctrine of the incarnation of the Word, the doctrine that the eucharist is indeed the body and blood of Christ, and the doctrine of the resurrection of the flesh, are interdependent. If one is denied, then the coherence of the whole economy falls apart.

[4] For the rest of the paragraph and for 5.2.3, the Greek text is found in a quotation in John Damascene, *Parallela*.

through creatures, for God furnishes us with what has been created, making the sun to rise and the rain to fall as God wills. [In keeping with this dispensation, he declares][1] that the cup which is of this creation is his blood, from which he gives increase to our blood, and that the bread which is of this creation is his body, from which he gives increase to our bodies.[2]

5.2.3: When, therefore, both the cup that has been mixed[3] and the bread that has been made, receive the word of God[4] and become the eucharist of Christ's body and blood[5], from which the substance of our flesh is increased and made consistent, how can they deny that flesh is capable of receiving the gift of God which is eternal life, [since] it is nourished by Christ's body and blood and is his member? As the blessed apostle says in his letter to the Ephesians: 'For we are members of his body, of his flesh and of his bones.'[6] He does not say this of some spiritual and invisible being, for a spirit has neither flesh nor bones [cf. Lk. 24.39], but of that arrangement which is true human nature, consisting of flesh and nerves and bones, and which is nourished from the cup, which is his blood, and gains increase from the bread, which is his body. Just as a cutting of wood from the vine planted in the ground fructifies in its season, or as a grain of wheat falling into the earth and decomposing, rises with manifest increase by the Spirit of God, who contains all things [cf. Wis. 1.7], and then, through the wisdom of God serves human use, and having received the word of God becomes the eucharist, which is Christ's body and blood, so also our bodies, being nourished by it, and deposited in the earth, and suffering decomposition there, shall rise at the appointed time, the Word of God granting them resurrection to the glory of God

[1] The words in parentheses are not actually in the text but seem to be required by the flow of the argument.

[2] Dogmaticians have often pointed to the almost Capharnaitic realism of these words, as though there were a material nourishment of human flesh and blood with the flesh and blood of Christ. The words however ought not to be taken too literally, but seen as a strong way of insisting that the eucharistized bread and wine do indeed become the body and blood of Christ and nourishment of the whole person, body and spirit. The manner of presence and communion has obviously to be in keeping with the reality of Christ's risen state. Irenaeus had no clear vocabulary whereby to express the specific nature of sacramental presence.

[3] This may well refer to the mixing of water with the wine.

[4] The word of God is most likely the eucharistic prayer. It might be argued that such a turn of phrase implies that the prayer incorporates the supper words of Jesus, but given present knowledge of early prayers this is not necessarily implied. It is also possible that Irenaeus implicitly associates the words spoken and the Word in whose name they are invoked.

[5] This is the way the Latin reads. The Greek in Damascene and the Armenian read:'the eucharist becomes Christ's body and blood'. The sense is not affected, since in both cases what is designated is that which has been blessed and through thanksgiving become the body and blood of Christ.

[6] The reference is probably to Eph. 5.29-30.

the Father, who freely gives to this mortal immortality, to this corruptible incorruptibility, because the strength of God is made perfect in weakness[1], lest we should ever become puffed up, as though we had life from ourselves, or exalt ourselves against God, our minds becoming ungrateful . . .

---

[1] In this rather complicated sentence, Irenaeus is clearly resorting to a number of biblical images to stress the reality of the resurrection of the flesh, of which not even death should allow us doubt. Thus he illustrates the resurrection of the flesh, nourished by the body and blood of Christ, and yet buried in the ground at death, by the example of the plant or the grain of wheat which planted in the earth and decomposing bring forth fruit. In other words, decomposition of the body is no argument against the resurrection. It will be given resurrection at the appointed time just as surely as, by divine disposition, the decomposed grain produces the ear of wheat.

He also shows the unity of God's economy through his metaphor. God creates the grain and the vine, which through death produce fruit; causes this fruit to become the body and blood in which the Word made flesh died and rose; and nourishes with it our human flesh which, though it must die, is saved by this food and drink from corruption and given immortality.

Conclusion

What emerges for a student of liturgy from a reading of these texts of Irenaeus may be summed up under three headings: (a) Baptism: rite and doctrine; (b) Eucharist: rite and doctrine; (c) worship and the rule of faith.

BAPTISM

1. The Rite of Baptism

The principal point for the liturgy of baptism is its connection with the rule of faith. The creed, as handed down by the apostolic tradition, is proclaimed in the baptismal rite. As known by Irenaeus, this proclamation seems to have consisted in the invocation of the names of Father, Son and Spirit over the candidate. Pre-baptismal catechesis followed the structure of this proclamation, fitted into the context of the history of salvation. If the *Proof of the Apostolic Teaching* does indeed serve as guideline for pre-baptismal catechesis, it is of interest that this did not exclude some direct discussion of baptismal rites.

Though anointing was practised in some churches at the time, this does not seem to have been done in the rites practised at Lyons. When Irenaeus mentions the mystical anointings of the gnostics associated with the redemption of the perfect, he has nothing to say about catholic anointings.

The candidates for baptism may be of any age and can include infants and children. This is one of the earliest clear testimonies to the practice of pedobaptism.

2. The Doctrine of Baptism

While Irenaeus enunciates the catholic doctrine of baptism, he does so in response to the exaggerations of the gnostics.

The most fundamental point is that baptism is not only for the remission of sins, but for regeneration into divine life. As such it includes the gift of the Spirit, which is the imprint of the images of the Father and the Son. The Spirit unifies the baptized in the unity of the one church into which baptism incorporates them, so that they are both a spiritual and a bodily communion. As seal of eternal life, baptism carries the guarantee of the resurrection of the flesh.

In elaborating this doctrine against the gnostics, Irenaeus teaches the one creation by the one God, the goodness of material creation, the incarnation of the Word in the birth of Jesus and so the identity of Jesus and Christ from the beginning rather than the descent of Christ on the man Jesus, and regeneration given to all at baptism.

EUCHARIST

1. Eucharistic Rites

The eucharist is celebrated according to the mandate of Christ at the Last Supper. It is celebrated in bread and wine, the latter mixed with water. It is celebrated with thanksgiving and invocation of the name of Christ over the bread and wine. The rite culminates in the eating and drinking of the eucharistized bread and wine.

The format of the eucharistic prayer is not clarified and invocation (*epiclesis*) may refer either to the whole prayer as done in the name of Christ, or to a section of the prayer which is invocation by way of distinction from that part which is thanksgiving.

What is learned from Irenaeus about the rites of the Marcosians may show ways in which they kept elements of early christian practice after they had been dropped by the orthodox. This would include a blessing prayer which is a prayer of invocation rather than of thanksgiving, and women's participation in such prayers.

While it is not included by Irenaeus in a eucharistic prayer, some of his expressions of the mystery of redemption influenced the prayer of the *Apostolic Tradition*. The image of Christ's conflict with death and the powers of the abode of death, and of the overcoming of darkness by light, may well have been taken from Irenaeus, who in turn reflects the paschal homiletic tradition.

2. The Doctrine of the Eucharist

The principal points of Irenaeus's teaching on the eucharist have to do with the sacramental reality of Christ's body and blood and with sacrifice.

The eucharist is celebrated according to the mandate of Christ given to the apostles and passed down by the elders. It commemorates his death and nourishes the faithful. The prayer of blessing or thanksgiving is rendered in invocation of the name of the Word made flesh. It is this which offers the bread and wine to God. It is the prayer, rather than the sole words of institution, which transforms the bread and wine offered into the body and blood of Christ.

In the sacrament, the blessed bread and wine are no longer common bread and wine, but the body and blood of Christ. These are nourishment not only for the spirit but also for the body, that is the whole person. They effect a union with the risen Christ and are guarantee of the resurrection of the flesh.

Irenaeus is emphatic that what is blessed is indeed the body and blood of the risen Lord, so that his flesh and blood mingle with that of the communicants. He strains for explanations of how this may be understood. The most simple statement is that they are no longer common brread and wine. He also speaks of the mixture of the heavenly and the earthly, seeming to offer some analogy between the union of the human and divine in the incarnation and the union of the risen Christ with the elements in the eucharist.

Irenaeus offers an early testimony to the doctrinee that the eucharist is a sacrifice. This belongas to the period of the transfer of Old Testament cultic terms to Christian realities. Several factors are included in his application of sacrifice to the eucharist. First, it involves an offering of the earthly realities of bread and wine, meet offering to the Creator since they are symbolicallly first-fruits of the earth. This offering is done with thanksgiving in the name of Christ, so that the thanksgiving over the elements is itself the sacrifice of the new covenant, offered by the church and transforming the elements into Christ's body and blood. The value of such offering by the faithful, in the communion of the church, is naught if it does not include the sacrifice or offering of a good Christian life, lived in obedience to the gospel. That such offering is possible, being the offering of the free, comes from redemption in Christ. Hence it is not an offering for sin, but one done by those redeemed from sin in order to express their gratitude and their union with God. Their capacity to offer sacrifice is one of the gifts of redemption, for in it they act as friends of God in making a gift in response to the gifts which they have received, both in creation and in redemption.

WORSHIP AND THE RULE OF FAITH

For Ireenaeus, the norm of orthodox teaching is that it is according to the rule of faith handed down from the elders, and it is to this that he appeals against the gnostics.

The rule of faith is embodied in liturgical rites, which thus stand as proof of the faith. This is especiallyy true of baptism, the context for the profession and proclamation of the faith. One may thus appeal to this profession against heretics. It is also embodied in more symbolic form in the water rite of baptism and the blessing of the bread and wine in the eucharist. The water rite is a washing of the body and shows that the body is included in regeneration into God. Since the eucharist is in bread and wine which nourish the body, Irenaeus in teaching the resurrection of the flesh can say that the eucharist confirms this teaching as the teaching confirms the eucharist.

This bodily element in liturgical rites is also testimony to the truth of the goodness of creation and to the truth of the incarnation. If the one God had not created the material as well as the spiritual, and had the Word of God not appeared in human flesh, material things would not have been included in the rites of the new covenant.

While Irenaeus does not express this thought, one sees how his explanation of the sacraments is influenced by his desire to support the doctrines of creation and redemption. One also sees how this explanation is shaped in controversy and how it is affected by the culture that gave rise to gnosticism. On the one hand right faith can be drawn from the rite, on the other the elaboration of the faith in catechetical teaching or apologetic includes elements drawn from the cultural world that in turn influence the cel;ebration of the rites and their expression of the rule of faith. There is a mutuality between the *lex orandi* and the *lex credendi*, rather than the strict dependency of one upon the other. Irenaeus not only enunciates the principle that worship and doctrine must correspond. He exemplifies it in showing how a tradition evolves through the organic interaction of teaching and liturgy. In that, his exemplification of the principle may go beyond his own enunciation of it.

Bibliography

TEXT

St. Irenaeus. Proof of the Apostolic Preaching, translated and annotated by Joseph S. Smith, S.J. (The Newman Press, Westminster, MD.; 1952, and Longmans, Green and Company, London: 1953).

Irénée de Lyon, *Démonstration de la Prédication Apostolique*, nouvelle traduction de l'Armaenien avec introduction et notes, par L. M. Froidevaux, Sources Chraetiennes 62 (aEd. du Cerf, Paris: 1959).

Sancti Irenaei, Episcopi Lugdunensis, Libros Quinque Adversus Haereses edidit W. Wigan Harvey, 2 volumes (Cambridge, 1858. Republished in 1965 by the Gregg Press Incorporated, Ridgewood, New Jersey).

The Ante-Nicene Fathers, translations of the Fathers down to A.D. 325, edited by Alexander Roberts and James Donaldson, vol. 1 (Edinburgh, 1867. American Reprint of the Edinburgh Edition by Wm. B. Eerdmans Publishing Company, Grand Rapids, 1981), pp.399-567.

Irénée de Lyon, Contre Les Hérésies, edition critique par Adelin Rousseau et Louis Doutreleau, Livre I, Tome II, Sources Chraetiennes 264; Livre II, Tome II, SC 294; Livre III, Tome II, SC 211; Livre IV, Tome II, SC 100; Livre V, Tome II, SC 153 (Paris: Editions du Cerf, 1979, 1982, 1974, 1965, 1969).

Sheerin, Daniel J., *The Eucharist, Message of the Fathers of the Church,* volume 7 (Michael Glazier, Wilmington, Delaware: 1986), pp.244-252 (for texts on the eucharist only).

STUDIES

Daly, Robert, *Christian Sacrifice. The Judeo-Christian Background Before Origen* (The Catholic University of America Press, Washington DC, 1978), pp.339-359.

Dollar, G. W., 'The Lord's Supper in the Second Century', in *Bibliotheca Sacra* 117 (1960), pp.144-154.

Hamman, Adalbert, 'Irenaeus of Lyons' in *The Eucharist of the Early Christians*, translated from the French by Matthew J. O'Connell (Pueblo Publishing Company, New York: 1978), pp.86-98.

Houssiau, A., 'Le Baptême selon Irénée de Lyon', *Ephemerides Theologicae Lovaniensis* 60 (1984), pp.45-59.

Joncas, J. M., 'Eucharist Among the Marcosians: A Study of Irenaeus' *Adversus Haereses* I, 13: 2', in *Questions Liturgiques* 71 (1990), pp.99-111.

Pagels, E. H., 'A Valentinian Interpretation of Baptism and Eucharist and its Critique of "Orthodox" Sacramental Theology and Practice', in *Harvard Theological Review* 65 (1972), pp.153-169.

Palachkovsky, V., 'La théologie eucharistique de S. Irénée, évêque de Lyon', in *Studia Patristica* 2 (1957), pp.277-281.

Radopoulos, P., 'Irenaeus on the Consecration of the Eucharistic Gifts', in *Kyriakon. Festschrift Johannes Quasten*, edited by Patrick Granfield (The Catholic University of America Press, Washington, D.C.: 1968), pp.844-846.

Unger, Dominic, 'The Holy Eucharist According to Saint Irenaeus', in *Laurentianum* 20 (1979), pp.103-164. In the course of this article, Unger gives his own English translation of the pertinent passages from Irenaeus.

Alcuin/GROW Joint Liturgical Studies

All cost **£3.50 (US $8)** in 1991

1987 TITLES

1. **(LS 49) Daily and Weekly Worship—from Jewish to Christian**
by Roger Beckwith, Warden of Latimer House, Oxford
2. **(LS 50) The Canons of Hippolytus**
edited by Paul Bradshaw, Professor of Liturgics, University of Notre Dame
3. **(LS 51) Modern Anglican Ordination Rites**
edited by Colin Buchanan, then Bishop of Aston
4. **(LS 52) Models of Liturgical Theology**
by James Empereur, of the Jesuit School of Theology, Berkeley

1988 TITLES

5. **(LS 53) A Kingdom of Priests: Liturgical Formation of the Laity: The Brixen Essays**
edited by Thomas Talley, Professor of Liturgics, General Theological Seminary, New York.
6. **(LS 54) The Bishop in Liturgy: an Anglican Study**
edited by Colin Buchanan, then Bishop of Aston
7. **(LS 55) Inculturation: the Eucharist in Africa**
by Phillip Tovey, research student, previously tutor in liturgy in Uganda
8. **(LS 56) Essays in Early Eastern Initiation**
edited by Paul Bradshaw, Professor of Liturgics, University of Notre Dame

1989 TITLES

9. **(LS 57) The Liturgy of the Church in Jerusalem** by John Baldovin
10. **(LS 58) Adult Initiation** edited by Donald Withey
11. **(LS 59) 'The Missing Oblation': The Contents of the Early Antiochene Anaphora**
by John Fenwick
12. **(LS 60) Calvin and Bullinger on the Lord's Supper** by Paul Rorem

1990 TITLES

13-14 **(LS 61) The Liturgical Portions of The Apostolic Constitutions: A Text for Students**
edited by W. Jardine Grisbrooke (March 1990)
This double-size volume provides in effect two of the Studies for 1990, and costs double price (i.e. £7.00 in England in 1991).

15. **(LS 62) Liturgical Inculturation in the Anglican Communion**
edited by David Holeton, Professor of Liturgics, Trinity College, Toronto (June 1990)
16. **(LS63) Cremation Today and Tomorrow**
by Douglas Davies, University of Nottingham (December 1990)

1991 TITLES

17. **(LS64) The Preaching Service—The Glory of the Methodists**
by Adrian Burdon, Methodist Minister in Rochdale (March 1991)
An historical account of the origins of the 'Preaching Service' in John Wesley's time.
18. **(LS65) Irenaeus of Lyon on Baptism and Eucharist**
Edited with Selection, Translation and Commentary by David Power, SJ (June 1991)
The sacramental liturgical material in Irenaeus, most of which is well known in its scattered character, is here brought together by a world-famous scholar.
19. **(LS66) Testamentum Domini**
Edited with Introduction, Translation and Notes by Grant Sperry-White, Department of Theology, University of Notre Dame (September 1991)
As this series of Joint Studies adds year by year to the supply in translation of patristic texts which relate to liturgy, so the need for the *Testamentum Domini* to be included has become clear, and the need is now met with this Study.
20. **(LS67) Texts of the early Roman Liturgy** (Probable Title)
Edited by Gordon Jeanes, Lecturer in Liturgy, University of Durham (December 1991)
A collection of basic texts touching upon the origins of the Roman Liturgy, with particular reference to contemporary evidence as to the actual character of the rites as presented or experienced.

THE ALCUIN CLUB

The Alcuin Club exists to promote the study of Christian liturgy in general, and in particular the liturgies of the Anglican Communion. Since its foundation in 1897 it has published over 130 books and pamphlets. Members of the Club receive some publications of the current year free and others at a reduced rate.

Information concerning the annual subscription, applications for membership and lists of publications is obtainable from the Treasurer, The Revd. T. R. Barker, All Saints' Vicarage, Highlands Road, Runcorn, Cheshire WA7 4PS (Tel. 0928–575 666).

PUBLISHING PLANS

The Alcuin Club has recently made a three-year arrangement with the Liturgical Press, Collegeville, whereby the old tradition of an annual Alcuin Club major scholarly study will be restored. The first title due under this arrangement is to be published in early 1992: Alastair McGregor, *Fire and Light: The Symbolism of Fire and Light in the Holy Week Services.*

It is likely that the Joint Liturgical Studies (see the list on the preceding page) will be reduced to three per annum from 1992, and the Alcuin Club subscription will then include the annual publication (as above) and the three Joint Liturgical Studies.

Previous Alcuin Annual titles

(obtainable through booksellers, or via Grove Books Limited, post-free).

1980 *The Communion of Saints* (by Michael Perham) S.P.C.K. £6.95
1981 *Daily Prayer in the Early Church* (by Paul Bradshaw) S.P.C.K. £6.95
1982 *Nuptial Blessing* (by Kenneth Stevenson) S.P.C.K. £10.50
1983 *The Godly Order* (by Geoffrey Cuming) S.P.C.K. £8.50
1985 *The Meaning of Baptism* (by Raymond Burnish) S.P.C.K. £10.50
1986 *Earth and Altar* (by Donald Gray) Canterbury Press £10.50

Also 'Alcuin Club Manuals'
No. 1 *The Eucharist* by Michael Perham) S.P.C.K. 1981, £2.25
No. 3 *Family Services* (by Kenneth Stevenson) S.P.C.K., 1981, £2.25

Recent Alcuin Titles

Towards Liturgy 2000: Preparing for the Revision of the Alternative Service Book (edited by Michael Perham) S.P.C.K. 1990, £4.95
Liturgy for a New Century (edited by Michael Perham) S.P.C.K. 1991, £6.50.

THE GROUP FOR RENEWAL OF WORSHIP (GROW)

This Group, originally founded in 1961, has for twenty years taken responsibility for the Grove Books publications on liturgy and worship. Its membership and broad aims reflect a highly reforming, pastoral and missionary interest in worship. Beginning with a youthful evangelical Anglican membership in the early 1970s, the Group has not only probed venturously into the future of Anglican worship, but has also with growing sureness of touch taken its place in promoting weighty scholarship. Thus the list of 'Grove Liturgical Studies' on the facing page shows how, over a twelve-year period, the quarterly Studies added steadily to the material available to students on patristic, reformation and modern scholarly issues in liturgy. In 1986 the Group was approached by the Alcuin Club Committee with a view to publishing the new series of Joint Liturgical Studies, and this now quarterly series is, at the time of writing, in its fifth year of publication, sustaining the programme of four Studies each year.

Between the old Grove Liturgical Studies and the new Joint Liturgical Studies there is a large provision of both English language texts adn other theological works on the patristic era. These are listed in a systematized way on the next page but one.

Since the early 1970s the Group has had Colin Buchanan as chairman and Trevor Lloyd as vice-chairman.

OTHER GROVE BOOKS PUBLICATIONS ON WORSHIP

GROW puts forward for publication once a quarter a cheaper 'Grove Worship Booklet', which is popular and pastoral in style, 24 pages in length, and £1.60 in sterling price in 1991. The Series has reached no. 117 mid-1991, and is in numerical continuity with the beginning of the original 'Grove Booklets on Ministry and Worship', of which no. 1 came in December 1971.

Recent titles include:

110 Worship in the Restorationist Movement by James Steven
111 Introducing Patterns for Worship by Trevor Lloyd, Jane Sinclair, Michael Vasey
112 Children in Communion by Colin Buchanan
113 But who will Preside? by Alan Hargave
114 Worship in Rural Areas by David Cutts
115 Readers and Worship in the Church of England by Carolyn Headley
116 Introducing Promise of His Glory by Trevor Lloyd, Jane Sinclair, Michael Vasey
117 Multi-Faith Worship and Christian Truth by David Bookless

Grove Books also publishes a monthly journal, *News of Liturgy,* edited by Colin Buchanan, which is the semi-official channel of information in the Church of England on liturgical subjects. It is sent by air also to subscribers all over the English-speaking world. Postal subscription (without quarterly studies or Booklets) in 1992: **£5.50** inland, **£8** by air overseas (US**$16**). There is also a quarterly *News of Hymnody.*

For postfree purchases or catalogue information write to Grove Books.

Grove Liturgical Studies

This series began in March 1975, and was published quarterly until 1986. Each title has 32 or 40 pages. Nos. 1, 3-6, and 10 are out of print. Asterisked numbers have been reprinted. Prices in 1991, £2.50

- *2 **LANGUAGE LITURGY AND MEANING** by Anthony Thiselton
- *7 **WHAT DID CRANMER THINK HE WAS DOING?** by Colin Buchanan
- *8 **HIPPOLYTUS: A Text for students with translation, notes and commentary** by Geoffrey J. Cuming
- 9 **LAY PRESIDENCY AT THE EUCHARIST?** Edited by Trevor Lloyd
- 11 **USING THE BIBLE IN WORSHIP** Edited by Christopher Byworth
- *12/13 **WORSHIP IN THE NEW TESTAMENT** by C. F. D. Moule (80 pages, £4.50)
- 14 **THE END OF THE OFFERTORY: An Anglican Study** by Colin Buchanan
- 15 **ESSAYS ON HIPPOLYTUS** edited by Geoffrey Cuming
- 16 **LITURGY AND SYMBOLISM** by Nicholas Sagovsky
- 17 **AUTHORITY AND FREEDOM IN THE LITURGY** edited by Kenneth Stevenson
- 18 **CHARLES SIMEON, PREACHER EXTRAORDINARY** by Hugh Evan Hopkins
- 19 **EUCHARISTIC OFFERING IN THE EARLY CHURCH** by Richard P. C. Hanson (28 pages)
- 20 **THE DEVELOPMENT OF THE NEW EUCHARISTIC PRAYERS OF THE CHURCH OF ENGLAND** edited by Colin Buchanan
- 21 **THE WESTMINSTER DIRECTORY OF PUBLIC WORSHIP** With an introduction by Ian Breward
- 22 **E. C. RATCLIFF: REFLECTIONS ON LITURGICAL REVISION** edited by David H. Tripp
- 23 **SYMBOLISM AND THE LITURGY (i)** edited by Kenneth Stevenson
- 24 **ADDAI AND MARI—THE ANAPHORA OF THE APOSTLES: A TEXT FOR STUDENTS** edited by Bryan Spinks
- 25 **MAKING THE LITURGICAL PSALTER** by David Frost
- 26 **SYMBOLISM AND THE LITURGY (ii)** edited by Kenneth Stevenson
- 27 **INFANT COMMUNION—THEN AND NOW** by David Holeton
- 28 **HE GAVE THANKS: AN INTRODUCTION TO THE EUCHARISTIC PRAYER** by Geoffrey Cuming
- 29 **THE LITURGICAL PORTIONS OF THE DIDASCALIA** edited by Sebastian Brock and Michael Vasey
- 30 **LUTHER'S LITURGICAL CRITERIA AND HIS REFORM OF THE CANON OF THE MASS** by Bryan Spinks
- 31 **EUCHARISTIC SACRIFICE—THE ROOTS OF A METAPHOR** by Rowan Williams
- 32 **WHOSE OFFICE? DAILY PRAYER FOR THE PEOPLE OF GOD** by David Cutts and Harold Miller
- 33 **ANGLO-CATHOLIC WORSHIP: An Evangelical Appreciation after 150 years** edited by Colin Buchanan
- 34 **EUCHARISTIC LITURGIES OF EDWARD VI: A Text for Students** edited by Colin Buchanan
- 35 **BACKGROUND DOCUMENTS TO LITURGICAL REVISION 1547-1549** edited by Colin Buchanan
- 36 **LITURGICAL PRESIDENCY IN THE EARLY CHURCH** by Paul Bradshaw (28 pages)
- 37 **WHY LITURGICAL WORSHIP ANYWAY?** by Michael Sansom
- 38 **THE LITURGY OF THE FRANKFURT EXILES 1555** edited by Robin Leaver
- 39 **LATEST LITURGICAL REVISION IN THE CHURCH OF ENGLAND 1978-1984** by Colin Buchanan
- 40 **ESSAYS ON EUCHARISTIC SACRIFICE IN THE EARLY CHURCH** edited by Colin Buchanan
- 41 **ANGLICAN EUCHARISTIC LITURGY 1975-1985** by Colin Buchanan
- *42 **A LITURGICAL GLOSSARY** compiled by Michael Sansom
- 43 **LITURGIES OF THE SPANISH AND PORTUGUESE REFORMED EPISCOPAL CHURCHES** edited by Colin Buchanan
- 44 **NURTURING CHILDREN IN COMMUNION: ESSAYS FROM THE BOSTON CONSULTATION** edited by Colin Buchanan
- 45 **FOURTH CENTURY ANAPHORAL CONSTRUCTION TECHNIQUES** by John Fenwick
- 46 **INCLUDE US IN—INCLUSIVE LANGUAGE IN LITURGY** by Vivienne Faull and Jane Sinclair
- 47 **THE MEDIEVAL GROWTH OF LITURGICAL SYMBOLISM** by Paul Rorem
- 48 **ANGLICAN CONFIRMATION** by Colin Buchanan

PATRISTIC STUDIES

Grove Liturgical Studies

(32 or 40 pages stapled) £2.50

ENGLISH TEXTS

8. **Hippolytus: A Text for Students, with Translation, Notes and Commentary** edited by Geoffrey Cuming (now in fourth impression)
24. **Addai and Mari: A Text for Students, with Introduction, Translation, and Notes,** edited by Bryan Spinks
29. **The Liturgical Portions of the Didascalia,** selected, translated and edited by Sebastian Brock and Michael Vasey

OTHER RELEVANT STUDIES in this SERIES

12/13. **Worship in the New Testament** by C. F. D. Moule (80 pages £4.50) This was the original Lutterworth Ecumenical Study in Worship, now twice reprinted in Grove Liturgical Studies.

15. **Essays on Hippolytus,** edited by Geoffrey Cuming, with essays on the text (see no. 8 in the Series listed above) by E. C. Whitaker (Baptism), Geoffrey Cuming (Eucharist), and Paul Bradshaw (Ordination)
19. **Eucharistic Offering in the Early Church,** by R. P. C. Hanson—a re-examination of the doctrine arising from the patristic texts.
31. **Eucharistic Sacrifice—The Roots of a Metaphor,** by Rowan Williams—a further re-exploration, with reference to Study no. 19 listed above.
36. **Liturgical Presidency in the Early Church,** by Paul Bradshaw—an expansion of a paper given to the Society for Liturgical Study.
40. **Essays on Eucharistic Sacrifice in the Early Church,** edited by Colin Buchanan—further papers, relating to nos. 19 and 31 above, from Michael Vasey, David Gregg, Kenneth Stevenson, and Rowan Williams.
45. **Fourth Century Anaphoral Construction Techniques,** by John Fenwick—an exploration of Eastern roots of eucharistic liturgy.